CALM

IN 40 IMAGES

Published in 2024 by The School of Life
First published in the USA in 2024
930 High Road, London, N12 9RT

Design @marciamihotichstudio
Printed in Lithuania by Balto Print

A proportion of this book has appeared online at
www.theschooloflife.com/articles

The School of Life publishes a range of books on essential topics
in psychological and emotional life, including relationships,
parenting, friendship, careers and fulfilment. The aim is always
to help us to understand ourselves better – and thereby to grow
calmer, less confused and more purposeful. Discover our full
range of titles, including books for children, here:
www.theschooloflife.com/books

The School of Life also offers a comprehensive therapy service,
which complements, and draws upon, our published works:
www.theschooloflife.com/therapy

ISBN 978-1-916753-00-6

10 9 8 7 6 5 4 3 2 1

Cover: Chase Dekker, *Horses Grazing,
Grand Teton National Park, Wyoming, United
States (detail), 2007*. Photo Chase Dekker
Wild-Life Images/Getty Images

CALM
IN 40 IMAGES

The School of Life

CONTENTS

INTRODUCTION

We've tried to picture where this book might be read. Perhaps in bed at a difficult hour, somewhere between three and five in the morning. You might have been trying to get back to sleep for a while now. Maybe you're in a hotel, in some kind of skyscraper with views onto a boundless foreign city. You might have picked the book up at an airport – Singapore or São Paulo – or been given it as a parting gift by a friend.

And the hope – as ever – is that it could in some ways make things lighter and easier; or at least less eerie and sad. It's a high ambition. We read so many books and, in the end, as with people, are marked by only a very few.

There's a lot of prestige around long books and even more around complicated-sounding ones. But as we're imagining the reader past the age of exams and wholly uninterested in intellectual boasting, this one will be neither.

There are a stream of pictures, but this is no standard art book. The words aren't trying to explain the images or elucidate a school of art; they're being invited to shed light on a theme – and to usher in a mood. They're there chiefly for their capacity to soothe and reassure. The odd one might spark a daydream or an association; it might hold your gaze for a moment and pave the way for a more hopeful train of thought. The true purpose of any book should – in the end – perhaps just be to try to leave the reader feeling a bit better.

We wrote this book because we've spent a lot of time feeling anxious ourselves. And also because, very slowly, we're getting less so. Certain ideas, endlessly repeated like an exercise regime, have helped. As have certain rituals of self-exploration, processing and discussion with therapists and friends.

A lover of calm isn't someone who is always perfectly serene; they are someone especially committed to an ideal, someone who never ceases to search for ways to hold on to perspective and recover a fragile sense of equanimity. We can legitimately count as lovers of calm when we ache for calm, not when we are calm all the time. Perhaps we'll be irritable again later today and panic tomorrow. What counts is the commitment – of which this book is a small indicator and ally.

We live in an age much impressed by drama and strenuous exertion. This book hopes to pull us in another direction, towards the more earnest, unheralded satisfactions of stability and serenity.

Living is something of an ongoing emergency. The task of art is to make things less unbearable day to day; the task of art is to help to calm us down.

THE WATER IS CALM, the horizon endless, the air warm. As we're being invited to realise, this is our true home, which doesn't mean that this is where we can be day to day. Far from it, but this is where we long to be; this is what our hearts crave; this is where we have been trying to get to all our lives.

We might attempt to look at the image for a whole minute – which is a very long time to look at anything – and to lose ourselves in the vastness. We can meander around the sky, the sea, the line where they meet and the gentle ripples in the foreground. This can be our destination; this is where we should remember to steer ourselves despite a panoply of distractions and futile and draining obligations. We will have succeeded if, after the tumult, we manage at last to be as it already is.

To put it at its grandest, calm is the meaning of life. By which is meant that calm is the thing that everything else should ultimately contribute to. Plenty of things are important and notable: money, friends, art, work. But if we probe hard at why they matter, if we push upstream, we eventually find that it's because of their power to contribute to something else, to what the Romans poetically knew as the *summum bonum*, the highest of all goods: a steady unruffled peaceful state of mind.

That calm ocean is calling to us; it should elicit in us an ache, and a sadness. It's where we belong but have spent so little time in until now; a realm at once foreign and intimately familiar – from which we are in exile.

At least the image can orient us, and lend us a more secure sense of our intended destination. This is where we will get to when – and if – we finally and truly win at life.

Hiroshi Sugimoto, *Caribbean Sea, Jamaica*, 1980

WE DESERVE TO FEEL SORRY FOR OURSELVES for the world we've built. We face unprecedented difficulties holding on to anything tranquil or soothing. We are continually – with the help of monstrous technologies – being goaded towards fury, excitement, panic and distraction. No hour of the day is free of reminders of where else we should be, what else we need to do and what may befall us if we are not extremely lucky or careful.

Other eras knew fear and disturbance too, of course. But there were an array of in-built dampeners that kept our forebears steady and that we have, without realising what we were doing, under a mistaken search for 'convenience', systematically dismantled. The walls between humans used to be more solid. We didn't hear each other's thoughts as loudly as we do now. We were less exposed to minute-by-minute discharges of envy and contempt. We didn't need to know everything that unfolded in the minds of everyone else. There were long quiet seasons. We loathed the boredom and the dull skies – but how they protected us and how mightily we may want them now. All those eventless hours when there was nothing to watch and nowhere to go were – far more than we ever knew – keeping madness and exhaustion at bay.

The loss of calm is very far from being all our fault. We are the victims of an age and of a devilish set of inventions – that began with steam and haven't stopped since. Those who came before us were not intrinsically any more mentally self-possessed; they were just (in this particular area at least) a lot more fortunate.

We may feel our agitations very personally but we should, in order to be appropriately compassionate and productively therapeutic, learn to interpret them also with immense historical awareness – and ensuing generosity.

Michele Nastasi, *Downtown Dubai*, 2015,
from the 'Arabian Transfer' series

PART OF OUR DIFFICULTY with staying calm is that we have such trouble understanding what we want – and those in charge of selling us things know our infirmities only too well.

Somewhere in our evolution, we failed to develop a robust facility for clearly distinguishing between idle desires – fancies and mirages – and true needs, substantial elements from which authentic happiness can be built. We didn't acquire an accurate capacity to discern what was essential from what was superfluous and so came to be as easily delighted by an ice cream as by a therapy session; a gold watch as a friendship; a pornographic website as a work of literature. Like an innocent child in a scary fairy tale, we put our soft hands in the paws of some very hungry wolves.

The massed ranks of advertisers appreciate with uncanny intelligence what we really need: they just don't want to sell it to us. They instead twin beautiful evocations of the true ingredients of contentment with a range of haphazard trinkets and baubles. We end up with clothes, but not the love we hoped might be delivered through them. We acquire watches and bags, but not the confidence and the self-possession we thought they'd usher in.

We suffer because peace of mind lacks an advertising agency. There are no talented advocates speaking up on its behalf to the world on a mass scale and, in their absence, we let ourselves forget who we are.

We should, to protect ourselves, realise our poor track record at holding on to our priorities – and our intense susceptibility to images of all kinds, the helpful ones and the beguiling and mischievous ones, waiting up there on street corners to excite, seduce and fool us.

Natan Dvir, *Zara 01*, 2008, from the 'Coming Soon' series

IN ALL PARTS OF THE WORLD, in pretty much all eras (save our own), our collective imaginations have liked to return again and again to the idea of paradise. Here, at last, the striving and the discord will come to an end; here, at last, we will be at peace. Most often, paradise has been imagined as a garden or a park, with streams, lakes, fruit trees, sunshine, docile animals, soft grass, tropical vegetation and a version of free love. It has also been – above all else – a place of calm. After all the worry and the meanness, we'll be able to lie down in the shade of a fig or a mango tree and watch a delicate cloud drift languidly across an azure sky. We'll take slow deep breaths of an air scented with the aromas of lavender and jasmine and we'll want for nothing.

It's a deep pity for us that we so quickly like to declare that we don't 'believe' in paradise. A disdain for the claims of organised religions should never coldly cut us off from the value of picturing other, better states. Our reveries aren't merely a waste of time; they're bracketing pain for a while, helping us to recharge for the battles ahead and enabling us to get a more secure handle on our true aspirations.

Even as hard-core atheists, we should learn to ask ourselves what our particular version of a non-spiritual 'paradise' would be like – and take regular imaginative rests there for a time. How would the place look? What would the view be of? Who would we be with? And what might be for lunch?

We already have versions of paradise in our minds waiting to be activated and explored. We don't need to die to go there – and we certainly don't need to believe. We just need to give ourselves permission more regularly to have one of the most innocent and recuperative of escapades: a daydream.

Thomas Cole, *The Garden of Eden*, 1828

IN A COMPLICATED WORLD, there remain few more delightful things than to closely observe – and ideally be in the physical company of – a sleeping baby. They seem so concentrated and so profoundly in love with the act of sleeping. They are doing such important work as they rest. Their tired minds have in the preceding hours been learning the next few pages of the gigantic manual of life: how water flows, how to make mummy smile or what fingers are. They might only have been on the planet for twelve-and-a-half weeks and already channels are being carved in the pristine wax tablets of their minds. In a few hours, they'll be alert and ready to go again. They'll try to suck your knuckle or put their toe in their eye. They'll gurgle adorably or wail because a door slammed unexpectedly. But for now, there is only an entirely mysterious journey through aeons of cosmic time and space.

We think we have so much to teach them but the traffic shouldn't be in one direction only. They are reminding us of the value of modest claims. We were like them once and will be so again towards the very end. They suggest we want for very little in our core. Some food, a warm place to lay our head, someone to stroke us, a gentle song and a chance to look up and see a kind-hearted face gazing benevolently at us.

We've made things hugely complicated for ourselves. We spend most of every day restless, angry and dissatisfied. Even sleep seldom restores us. There's always part of our minds that is alert and untrusting, fearful and vigilant. We buy our so-called maturity at a very high cost.

We should acknowledge the scale of our longings: how much we might want to be bathed, swaddled and put comfortably down for a very long nap somewhere cosy and undemanding; how much we want to return to some of what we used to know so well.

kledge, *Sleeping Baby*, 2009

ALL DAY LONG, we are in conversation with other people. The chatter can be remorseless, draining and tyrannical. But its greatest cost stems from the way it makes us forget to commune with someone very close by who has extremely important things to say to us, namely of course, us. Unfortunately, our deep selves aren't very good at speaking up. They need a lot of quiet, encouragement, softness and understanding in order to begin to reveal their concerns.

They are shy because so much of what they have to disclose threatens to be embarrassing, vulnerable or just contrary to what's expected of us. Perhaps they are upset about a little laugh our partner let out eight hours ago in the kitchen; maybe they're concerned with something someone briefly mentioned at the office at lunchtime or they might be unable to forget a vindictive line in a sarcastic article they scanned for an instant on the train. We are – regrettably – a great deal more sensitive than we ever like to imagine. Anxiety is the by-product of an accumulation of unprocessed worries and regrets. The less we give ourselves opportunities to unpack our true concerns, the more we will be filled with a general, non-specific background sense of alarm. And the less introspection we have done, the more the prospect of solitude is likely to fill us with dread. We can be sure that we have accumulated a host of unthought thoughts when our own company starts to feel simply unbearable.

We need – once the external noise has faded away – to turn inwards and interview ourselves. We need to go back over our days, sifting through their minutiae, in search of what is surreptitiously powering our disturbances of mind.

There will be so much less to be anxious about once we have given ourselves the opportunity to map our true worries.

Mark Salamon, *Going Down*, 25th August, 2016. From the
'Sunsets from the Backyard' series, 2020–present

– Wait until the noise of the day has subsided. Find a quiet room. Probably lie in bed – or in the bath.

– Close your eyes and open the iris of inner awareness wide. Ask yourself: *What am I deep down worried about now?* Don't rush to find an answer. Take it very slowly. Wait for something to emerge rather than reaching for an insincere plausible first notion. Let your gut speak rather than your day-to-day conscious intelligence; it has a much better sense of these things. It will tend to yield material that won't make immediate sense. It might be someone's name or a still image taken at some point during the day by the mind's camera.

– Unpack the name or image. What is it that's so worrying here? Let your gut tell you; it knows but it isn't its style to speak up clearly. It might give its answer in alarmed broad brushstrokes because it has a young side to it.

– Allow adult reason to intrude. Start a dialogue between the gut and reason. Level questions that sweetly take issue with panic and refuse to let alarm have the last word.

Ask: *What – really – is there to be afraid of here?* What is the worst that could happen? What are they most likely to be saying?

– Feel a measure of perspective return. Systematically, shine a bright light on every possible anxiety currently in the mind's chamber. Probe at scenarios repeatedly to weaken their strangeness and their hold. Worries only stay powerful if they stay ignored and unnamed. With the patience of an angler, pull them carefully into consciousness, one catch at a time, and get to know them exhaustively. Dialogue about them for as long as is needed to drain them of their power. Learn to make anxieties old news; familiarise and bore yourself into serenity.

– Repeat every night and, for the particularly fragile among us, every couple of hours.

Mark Salamon, *Lomo Glow*, 20th November, 2018. From the
'Sunsets from the Backyard' series, 2020-present

WE WANTED SO MUCH TO VISIT and eventually got to the island, at huge expense and with considerable physical exertion. It was one of the finest times of our lives: calm, liberating and hopeful. But that was a while ago now, three and a half years, and rarely do we think back to those five days, even though the photos are somewhere on our phone, a long scroll away. In so far as we ever still consider the holiday, it's in terms of a future prospect. We might – with any luck – manage to go back there, or somewhere nearby, the summer after next.

We are, without ill intent, being phenomenally wasteful with our redemptive moments. There are treasuries inside us that we never revisit, there are riches that it doesn't occur to us to reconsider. We insist – with blind literalness – that the only way to travel is to go to the airport. Yet the mind forgets almost nothing. It stores within its dense folds pretty much everything that we have ever experienced – the feel of the cool painted tiles in the house in Santorini, the smell of the mint leaves in the garden in Norfolk, the honey and yoghurt on the terrace in Normandy. All that is required for our memories to return to life is a prompt.

Nothing has disappeared: the mist over the mountains in Lucerne, that first morning in Beirut, the smell of heat and jet fuel at the airport in Lanzarote, the honey and bread with poppy seed left for us by the owner of the cottage in Corfu. We don't need to buy things to make them ours or arduously put our physical selves on a bit of the earth to know them. We travel best and fastest in our minds – as art and literature have always known.

Something becomes ours again every time we summon it mentally and the more intimately we can imagine it, the more it will relive in us. We can right now be on the rocky sun-bleached cove, looking out to the white windmills, with the salt on our skin and the prospect of a day without obligations and burdens. Nothing can stop us from more actively engaging with the calm and beauty we have already known. We have a lot more freedom than we may have feared and suspected.

Giannis Giannelos, *Greece*, 2017

THE MOST REVERED POEM in Japanese literature was written around 1686 by Matsuo Bashō – and is, famously, only three lines long:

Old pond
a frog jumps in –
the sound of water

In the haiku tradition, a poet is only ever expected to do a part, and not even the greatest part, of the work of a piece of literature. Their task is to fashion the most evocative prompt – and then the rest is left to the reader who, by meditating on a few exquisitely selected words, has an opportunity to see reality afresh through the prism of their own lives and eyes. Our imaginings will, if we concentrate deeply enough on a haiku (and it would not be thought strange to spend half an hour daydreaming on one), invariably be superior to anything that someone else can detail for us. The task of literature is not for one person to give another their most precious experiences fully formed; it is for an outsider to provide us with the tools with which to fire up our own minds.

We can – with due and enormous respect – imagine extending this tradition to a series of prompts, free of all literary pretension, with the specific intent of focusing our minds on the key ingredients of calm and rest. Each of these would, without any literary claims, try to shift consciousness back to a serenity that is within us all but that we lose sight of in ordinary life:

– a little cottage in a valley/someone who cares/ kindness, sympathy
– a hot deep bath/quiet in the house/a free mind
– in bed late at night/no more obligations/a return to ourselves
– heavy rain/the smell of the earth/memories
– a long flight/the desert below/new beginnings.

The Japanese tradition takes a highly optimistic view of us, the readers. We have the necessary experience. We have the scenes in us all along: frogs and ponds but also quiet evenings, peaceful dawns, tender-hearted friends, reassuring cuddles and new-found courage. We have the calm we need inside us already.

All we need is to give ourselves the time and the context to pull scenes together in our minds – and to immerse ourselves in them with suitable focus. We have known how to be calm all along; we've just never before been so intently asked to imagine ourselves into feeling so.

Fujiwara no Teika, *Poems on Flowers and Birds of the Twelve Months* (detail), 18th century

THERE IS A TRADITION within the Christian church of training ourselves to ask, especially at moments of particular difficulty: *What would Jesus do now?*

This unusual exercise picks up on an observable phenomenon of the mind. Once we have read and seen enough of someone, we can without too much difficulty surmise the sort of things they would be likely to say in response to a situation. We may not be experts in the gospels but we can tell well enough what a loving, tender, forgiving Jesus-like move would be. We just don't generally have recourse to it, because the idea doesn't enter our minds, because we aren't trained to consciously model ourselves on anyone and therefore don't imagine we even have an option to improve on our first, generally more frantic and egoistic impulses.

What is poignant is that this doesn't mean we aren't modelling ourselves on someone; it's simply that the process of modelling isn't conscious. In truth, the way we speak to ourselves and others is continuously yet unconsciously derived from the way in which people used to speak around us when we were growing up. And, unfortunately for us (and those who have to live in our vicinity), these people were rarely paragons of maturity and serenity. Without knowing it, we bring some of the anger and drama of our forebears into play in a present that seldom deserves them.

The Christian exercise is ripe for secular re-adaptation. We should – at small and large moments – intentionally train ourselves to ask: what would a kind, calm and mature person do or say now? We can summon this person at will; they merely normally lack encouragement and a platform. When we are about to lose our tempers, they should smile kindly at us and say 'not now'. When we feel ourselves ready to make an unfair accusation, they should gently counsel a break and a walk outside.

We can't be responsible for the way others used to speak to us; but we can endeavour to moderate and modulate the voices we have recourse to henceforth – and therefore come more regularly to ask ourselves, as we prepare to slip into meanness and fretfulness: what would someone less agitated and wounded than me do now?

The healthy adult we need to lean on is already inside us. We just need to prompt them to speak then listen to them closely when they do so.

Antonello da Messina, *Christ Blessing*, 1465

WE'RE PROBABLY SO USED to the idea that we cease to note either its peculiarity or its originality. One of the world's main religions – the fourth most popular, with over 500 million followers, or around 7% of the global population – has as its chief symbol and most instantly recognisable token the head of a very calm-seeming man.

This head shows a little variation depending on where it was made. In south-east Asia, especially towards Malaysia and Indonesia, the eyes grow more elongated. In northern India, the brows are thicker and in eastern China the cheeks fleshier. But the essence of the message is identical; here is someone who worked out a way to conquer anxiety. Or, to put it at its simplest: follow me, and you too will be calm.

Other religions have made different promises to their followers: eternal life, earthly riches, divine favour, bodily recovery. Buddhism narrows the target substantially. As all those exquisite heads attest, what is first and foremost on offer here is serenity.

Without us even approaching the content of Buddhism, this emphasis should stop us in our tracks. If we could be granted one, and only one, wish, what we should perhaps really be asking for is calm. It's all very well trying to live forever or to levitate, but it's even better to be able to get through today and tomorrow without panic.

To back up its promises, Buddhism relies on a complex cosmology: we are an illusion; the self is not real; 'I' is a fiction; time does not exist. The ideas are dazzling and, from some perspectives, liberating too. But it's Buddhism's first and least specific point that deserves the greatest share of our attention. Here is a belief system founded by an Indian prince who committed himself – as very few others before and after him have done – to attempting to slay the dragon of anxiety. He understood how worry destroys everything and strove to endow calm with extraordinary glamour; his imperturbable face is there to remind us of our deepest yet too often neglected aspiration.

Following the example of Buddhism, we might devote ourselves in our own particular ways to the business of calming down, using whatever worked best for us (it might be psychotherapy, novels or Western philosophy). We might not want to become Buddhists, but – with the prince's sublimely tranquil example in mind – we might gain renewed determination to become *Calmists*.

Head of a Buddha, Gupta period,
late 5th–early 6th century

THE MODERN WORLD IS NEVER VERY KEEN to encourage us to make choices. We can – it tells us blithely – raise families and, at the same time, have flourishing careers. We can achieve tremendous things at the office, and keep our bodies in ideal shape. We can be ethical and successful. This is meant to be kind but it ends up being a cruelty all of its own.

It would be more honest and a lot more useful to admit to a darker reality: we need to choose. We cannot run a philharmonic orchestra and be a great and ever-present parent. We cannot be remorselessly effective in the workplace and constantly act with benevolence and kindness. And we definitely can't be completely calm and, concurrently, accumulate worldly riches and social renown. Something has to give – and it invariably does.

This starkness helps us precisely because there are so few public reminders of life's necessary trade-offs. Yet once we understand the incompatibilities, we are in a better position to do what we always needed to do: choose. With life's incommensurate aspects more clearly in view, we can end up in a position to sound out our own values and rank our priorities accordingly.

A noisy life has a range of specific upsides: glamour, fame, sex, triumph, thrill. And – of course – some downsides too: panic, exhaustion, fear, restlessness, mental collapse. Equally, a calm life has some lovely things going for it – rest, perspective, ease, contentment – while also threatening us with grave negatives: boredom, marginalisation, envy and emptiness.

The point is that we have to make a choice, and the more we see things as a choice, the less we will need to be surprised or let down by encounters with the downsides. If we aim for calm, we'll have done so without sentimentality. We'll know exactly what those rather empty days are protecting us against; we'll have openly chosen repose over drama, and mental well-being over the threat of breakdown. Naturally, at points, we'll rue the downsides. We'll feel wretched the day an old university acquaintance reveals they sold their company for a fortune or that there's a party going on in town to which we were not invited. These things sting. But we'll have acquired the ultimate safeguard. We'll know – in a way our societies never help us to – that we faced a choice and took it; we'll know we chose calm with our eyes open.

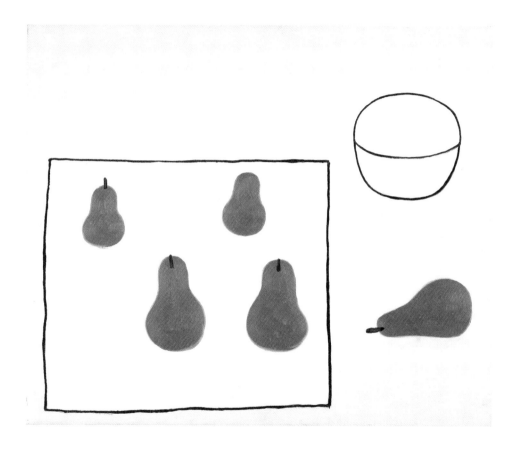

William Scott, *An Orchard of Pears, No. 7*, 1976-1977

AMONG THE YORUBA PEOPLE, an ethnic group of over 40 million spread between Nigeria, Togo and Benin, one of the most flattering ways to describe a person is to say they have much *itutu*. The word denotes a particular approach to life: unhurried, composed, assured and unflappable. If a bus is late, a person of *itutu* won't shout or get in a dispute with a ticket vendor; they'll let out a minor sigh and pull a weary smile. If the skies open just when they've laid out chairs in the garden for a party, they will – in their normal tranquil and unaffected way – simply take them all back in again. There isn't much that should rattle a person of *itutu*.

Crucially, *itutu* isn't any sort of divine gift or chance trait. It's a quality that can be cultivated and is the outcome of having absorbed a particular view of existence. For the Yoruba, agitation and anger flow from a mistaken and over-ambitious sense of what it lies in our power to alter. It's when we believe that we are more in command of external reality than we actually are that we respond to reversals and frustrations with rage. The calm person of *itutu* may be every bit as sad as their hysterical counterpart about the delayed bus or torrential shower, but what underpins their equanimity is a sense that trouble could not be skirted and must be accepted as belonging to the order of things. In their noble resignation, a person of *itutu* displays a grasp of another key term in Yoruba philosophy: *àṣẹ*, which we might translate as destiny, existence, or the cosmic order. What lies in the province of *àṣẹ*, can't be altered by any human will, but an enlightened person should understand the direction of *àṣẹ* and then adjust their desires and ambitions accordingly.

There is an important detail here: *itutu* doesn't only render a person wise. It additionally makes them attractive, including physically attractive, and what we might call 'cool' – which is why any self-respecting young Yoruba will strive hard to adopt its outward signs, particularly when a distinguished local photographer like Rachidi Bissiriou has offered to take one's portrait.

Many cultures retain a lingering suspicion that being effective might rely on a capacity to be frantic and hot-tempered. For the Yoruba, agitation isn't merely an offence to a proper understanding of the universe; it's also horribly unfashionable.

Rachidi Bissiriou, *Young Wife and Mother*, 1983

ONE OF THE REASONS why we are a good deal more worried than we should be is that we refuse to give our worries the kind of close-up focused attention they need in order to dissipate. We assume that we are attending to our worries, because they fill our minds, but there is an immense difference between being obsessed by a worry and taking it apart rationally piece by piece. We can be preoccupied by a topic without ever actually reflecting on it.

Whenever we feel an anxiety begin to gnaw at us, we should immediately clear time to worry exclusively and properly about it. We must force our minds to get very specific indeed about how a given problem could apparently 'ruin our lives' and discern any implausible dimensions a catastrophic scenario might have acquired in our imaginations. As we strive to name the worst in great detail, some of the more outlandish aspects of our fears will by necessity come to light – and can then be allayed by reason.

Every alarming situation involves an oscillation between a hope and a terror. We should calm ourselves by ceasing to hope for a moment – in order to look our terror bravely in the face. We should ask: even if disaster somehow came to pass, how survivable could it be? Of course we'd like things to go well, but could the worst be borne? We might be jobless, friendless, disgraced and an outcast. Yet how could life nevertheless go on? Far more than we're inclined to believe, it would almost certainly be possible to survive despite our losses. Every day, people agree to continue without a limb or a key organ, a loved one or social status. What we think we need is very different from what we could actually bear. We're a lot more resilient than we assume.

Peace of mind doesn't come from hoping for the best; it comes from close-up attention to the very worst – and from the sure knowledge that we can, with the strength we have inside us already, endure whatever fate might assign us.

J. M. W. Turner, *The Fall of an Avalanche in the Grisons*, exhibited 1810

OUR RELATIONSHIPS TEND TO BE far more turbulent than they should be because of a misleading background sense that a bond between two people can safely be assumed to be solid on the basis of a few significant moves having once been made: a marriage, a joint mortgage or a newborn baby.

Yet from a less sanguine perspective, no bond should ever be deemed unbreakable without being checked in on every few days. At any point, things can be said that could lead one or both parties to doubt the whole seemingly solid edifice. There is no such thing as a stable – in the sense of maintenance-free – union. Vigilance should be an invariable requirement.

Two questions in particular can rapidly descend on partners and fatefully gnaw away at their affections. Firstly: do they actually really love me? And secondly: are they really a good, kind, love-worthy person? Such enquiries may seem to have been answered fifteen years back, at that delightful little chapel on the seashore with twenty friends, or perhaps at their birthday eight months ago when we bought them a jumper, but our hearts are far more skittish and demanding than that. A missing word in the kitchen or an unattended chore can be enough to unleash a chain of anxieties.

We continually acquire little vexations that can make us question the other's sincerity or decency. And, like a pebble in a shoe, a small fear or misgiving can – if left unattended – gradually cause carnage. To protect our couples, we should get into a twofold habit. Firstly, enquiring – with a mutual vow not to grow angry or defensive, 'how might I have hurt you?' And then, without the slightest note of accusation and with an assurance that we will be heard with sincerity, we should have the chance to say 'this is how you have hurt me ...'

Love never dies mysteriously. It dies because microscopic disappointments have not been identified and cleared in time to prevent them coalescing into boulders.

Sunil Gupta, *Charlie and Pablo*, 1985,
from the 'Lovers: Ten Years On' series

UNFORTUNATELY FOR EVERYONE, we go around the world with scripts in our minds. A script is a collection of expectations about how events will unfold and how we should best respond to them – built up out of the worst moments of our childhoods and our most immature and frightened deductions from them. Here are some representative scripts: *when I make a mistake... I will get shouted at uncontrollably. Therefore, I must never admit I'm at fault. When I trust someone ... they betray me. Therefore, I must never open up. If I get too emotional, there will be chaos. Therefore, I must be very stern and detached. If a partner is out of contact for a while ... it means they've abandoned me. Therefore, I need to flare up at any threat of absence.*

These scripts tell us a lot about our pasts, but the tragedy is that, unaware they exist, we let them determine our futures. We insistently layer them onto situations in the here and now that could have had far more benevolent endings. A boss very gently points out a mistake and, out of a fear that this is a prelude to relentless humiliation, we snap back. Our partner lets us down in a minor way and, sure this means they are about to destroy us, we start to insult them.

The solution is to recognise that there can be different endings. *Yes, I made a mistake, but the result doesn't have to be cruel reprimand. Yes, the partner let me down, but they can – and do – still love me very much. I could get annoyed, but the emotion doesn't have to escalate uncontrollably.*

In other words, what happened originally doesn't have to keep happening. But only if we can first understand what actually happened. And to help us with this, we should explore the past by completing the following sentences: *when I make a mistake ... When I trust someone ... If I get too emotional ... If a partner has to be out of touch for a while ...*

The end goal of maturity might be defined as the ability to approach as much of life as possible without a script.

Jessica Todd Harper, *Self Portrait with Christopher
(living room)*, 2001, from the 'Interior Exposure' series

TOO OFTEN, WE IMAGINE OURSELVES as helpless before other people's anger. They threaten to go from frustration to outright annoyance without us having any opportunity to slow them down – or usher in a more nuanced approach.

But in truth, there is no mystery as to why conflicts escalate or, conversely, wind down. We can, at any moment, if we want to, tame the angriest tiger. The genie of rage can be snuffed out at will. We need only rely on two key moves.

The first involves saying, loudly and clearly: 'I hear you'. It's an error to suppose that angry people need their problems fixed; what they principally require is for someone to show them sustained and careful sympathy for having such problems. Their rage masks a fear of being abandoned. It's the world's apparent indifference that fuels their expletives. They want their pain to echo to another continent because they aren't sensing any response closer to home. It's the seeming deafness that's making them scream. They could live without an answer; what they can't bear is to have to do so without company.

Secondly, we need to paraphrase their complaint. It isn't enough to say that we hear them. We need to demonstrate that we really do so – which best occurs when we can skilfully put their grievance into slightly different words, a transposition that proves that we have been listening step by step to their foundational outburst. If our angry companion were to shout that we always forget the milk, we could calmly respond: 'I am hearing that the way I've forgotten to get us something for breakfast has been a real disappointment to you.' Or when they scream that we never let them know what we're doing in the evenings, we can say: 'I'm properly appreciating now that my scheduling failures have left you no room to plan things for yourself.' We don't need to say we're sorry; reflexive listening proves that we are so.

We can remain calm even if someone sees the world very differently to us or has caused us a host of inconveniences and discomforts. Anger isn't in the end to do with a frustration of our will; it's an agonised complaint about feeling alone.

Athapet Piruksa, *Lightning in rice field*, c. 2012

IT'S TYPICALLY ASSUMED that the goal of any educated and ambitious person will be to try to understand ever more about everything: the wiser we are, the more we will strive to know. But there's a contrary tradition in many philosophies and religions that points us to a very different and far more calming moral: that, at a certain moment, the wise will stop trying to understand who they are, why they are here and what everything means and surrender instead to 'the ineffable', that which cannot be grasped by anything as limited and flawed as the human mind.

In their mystical branches, Buddhism, Hinduism, Christianity, Judaism and Islam all stress that the greatest questions cannot be properly answered by human beings – and that silence and submission are the only fair ultimate responses to the *mysterium tremendum*, the awesome mystery at the heart of everything. We cannot possibly ever know our true purpose, the nature of existence, the role and relevance of the cosmos or the mind of God – and should not exhaust ourselves or offend truth by seeking to do so. In Mahāyāna Buddhism, ultimate reality is simply beyond articulation by an instrument as paltry as language. In Islam, the wise will capitulate to *Al-Ghaib*, what is divinely 'hidden' and 'incomprehensible', and the most pious Jews will not dare to utter the word 'God' from a sense that no human tongue should try to name *ein-sof*, the power that is conclusively beyond fathoming.

Via the concept of the ineffable, we are – unusually and kindly – being given permission not to understand. Our not-knowing – who we are, why we have been placed here and what we should be doing – does not have to be equated with error or laziness; it can be evidence of the noblest kind of humility before the unnameable nature of ultimate reality.

When we come up against barriers to our comprehension, we do not have to rail against our blindness. Instead, inspired by ancient philosophies, we can exchange fretful ambition for a serene resignation before the ungraspable beauty and complexity of all that we are fated by our limited minds never to be able to make sense of. We can at times willingly let go of our enervating pride and admit – through our silence – that we simply and blessedly do not know.

Hasegawa Tōhaku, *Pine Forest*, c. 1595

I AM R136A1, a gigantic Wolf-Rayet star residing – invisible to the naked eye – in the Tarantula Nebula of the Large Magellanic Cloud, a dwarf galaxy companion to the Milky Way, which despite measuring 32,200 light-years in diameter, can only be spotted as the faintest, most minuscule smudge on the clearest of nights in the southern sky.

Located approximately 157,000 light-years away from Earth, it would take you millions of years to reach me by your fastest spacecraft. When you did, you'd find that I was burning at around 46,000°K (Kelvin), eight times as hot as your sun, and that winds roared around me at 3,000 kilometres per second.

When I look east, I can see the 30 billion or so stars that make up the Large Magellanic Cloud, with its 60 globular clusters and 400 planetary nebulae. Gazing straight ahead, I sense the presence of the Milky Way, 13.6 billion years old, 100,000 light-years across, a collection of some 400 billion stars and planets which, in a minor and less densely populated region known as the Orion-Cygnus Arm, a mere 3,500 light-years across and approximately 10,000 light-years in length, somewhere houses the tiniest of blue dots in a corner of which you're reading this.

There is so much I don't know about you. I am oblivious to the tectonic shifts that sculpt your landscapes, the emergence of basic life some 3.5 billion years ago, and the intricate molecular dance within the 30 or so trillion cells that make up your body.

I am entirely indifferent to your concerns, your political turmoils, your regrets and the anger you harbour against your late mother. My role is different. I am here to offer a cosmic perspective, and to remind you that in the 93-billion-light-year expanse of the observable universe, you are a mercifully and gloriously inconsequential phenomenon destined imminently to be subsumed into the peace of eternal nothingness.

Large and small magellanic clouds, as seen from an
observatory in Chile's Atacama Desert (R136a1, if
you had eyes that could see it, would be somewhere
on the top left), 2011

A 'TRANSCENDENTAL EXPERIENCE' – from the Latin *transcendere*, meaning 'to go beyond' – denotes a brief, uncommon, ecstatic and revelatory period. During such a period we are able to loosen our hold on our characteristically narrow ego-specific concerns to identify with a totality that is larger, older, deeper than we are, and thus come out of it feeling intensely unburdened and liberated.

We might have a transcendental experience early on a summer's morning, looking at the mist starting to burn up in the valley below us, or late at night with the galaxies above us. We might go through one in a plane crossing the icefields of northern Canada or at 3 a.m., alone in a foreign hotel bedroom, contemplating matters from a new unbound perspective. Nature is especially good at prompting transcendental moments as are nights, solitude, the sounds of flutes, sitars and harps, airplanes, fevers, William Blake, Rumi, mountains and psilocybin and mescaline.

In the grip of a transcendental experience, who we are, the mistakes we have made, and how halting our uncertain trajectory has been matter less. We willingly let go of the compromised 'I' and all its often petty and mean-spirited obsessions in order to become, for a privileged while, a part of the timeless, beatific whole. We are the clouds, the rocks, the beetle climbing arduously up the bark of a tree, a baby being born on another continent, a nonagenarian breathing their last breath, a line in a poem and a star expiring in a distant galaxy. We don't care that we have been betrayed in love, were defeated at work and roughly handled in childhood. Our own death becomes a matter of utter indifference; we feel honoured to be occupying such a small space in the order of things and that we will soon disappear without a trace. We let go of it all in the name of an identification with the totality of existence. We willingly exchange ourselves for engulfment in otherness.

We have not gone mad. We'll be doing the school run or the accounts again in a few hours. But what counts is that we have accessed – and can now bookmark – a kind of experience that will always be on hand in memory as a rebuke to our most frantic, frightened or vain moments. It is the greatest privilege accorded to us by our complex minds that we do not always have to be simply and punishingly ourselves.

Albert Bierstadt, *Among the Sierra Nevada, California*, 1868

CONSTRUCTION OF COLOGNE CATHEDRAL began in 1248; the choir was consecrated in 1322 and work on the transepts got going in the late 1300s. However, a range of delays meant that it wasn't until the 1800s that the nave was completed, and the front twin towers started to rise – and it was 1996 before the south transept window was put in. Having required the labour of an estimated 150,000 people over almost 800 years, the cathedral was conclusively finished in 2007, with the completion of a new stained-glass window by the German artist Gerhard Richter.

Many of us have lives that sometimes feel as haphazard as that of a nameless stonemason chiselling a few blocks of limestone on Cologne Cathedral at some stage in the late 15th century: we know we're not getting anywhere fast and won't see any notable return before our deaths.

But when despair stalks us, we should – like that mason – step back and imagine ourselves as part of a larger whole that can redeem us through its scale, logic and beauty. However apparently inconsequential our daily labours may seem, we are also likely to be contributing to a larger endeavour comparable in nobility and honour to a cathedral: the pursuit of human knowledge, the economic development of a nation, the safe nurture and growth of another generation.

Even if we are only making the snacks or cleaning the tools of those actively engaged in such work, we are – by necessity – involved in a magisterial task too; we just forget to notice the fact. We need to perceive where, and how, we fit in and liberate ourselves from the punishing idea that we have to be the sole authors of a creation bearing our names, neatly completed within our lifetimes, in order for our work to have any value.

It is a folly to imagine that each of us must, in the course of the 50 or so years in which we are active in the world, make our own utterly distinctive mark on the order of things. We can happily be only a small paragraph, even a word or two, in a story running to millions of pages assembled by numberless nameless scribes over a succession of generations. We just need, to rescue ourselves from sadness, to remember and see more clearly the 'cathedral' we are building.

Johannes Franciscus Michiels, *Construction of the Cathedral, Cologne,* with the medieval crane still in place, 1855

WE ARE UP HERE OSTENSIBLY in order to get somewhere else fast. But the real destination lies not so much in another continent as in other, less familiar parts of ourselves.

We are out of our minds with boredom. All we have had for company for several hours now is a perspective onto an endless skyscape abutting in hazy infinity. Occasionally we glimpse a stretch of slate grey ocean or an implausibly vast icefield. Regions of the earth we had never suspected pass by without comment or notice.

The real point of this journey and its constraints lie in an invitation to self-exploration. We are being given – at last – encouragement to think, to open up areas of unthought experience and to unpick sequences of worries that have been pushed to the back of our minds as a result of our packed schedules.

We can ask ourselves a range of unusual questions. What am I really trying to do? Is this relationship working? What do I want of the next few years? What will have mattered at the end? Why do I worry so much? What could help me to be the person I want to be? How could I be good? To whom should I say sorry? How could I become a better version of me?

We might, at some stage, be tempted to pull out a pen and paper or make notes on our phone. As we do so, our minds seem less frightening and confused places. We can draw up lists. We can sketch the future. We identify our real concerns. We're working properly at last. We're doing maintenance we have shirked for far too long.

We will be able to be calm later on because we have – for a few hours – cleared away little tendrils of worry. We'll be able to sleep because our ideas won't be seeking revenge for having been ignored.

We realise how hard it is to think ordinarily, how much we have avoided it, and how much we are being helped by the passing view, by the sound of the engines (that evoke some of the soothing throbs of the womb) and by our constriction and isolation.

We complain so bitterly at how long we have to be cooped up here, but we are being gifted something very precious. We've been sent to the closest thing our times know to a monastery, a closeted faraway place from which we can hope to return with renewed insight, seriousness and courage.

We thought the flight was taking us elsewhere; if we have been good to ourselves, we will have stumbled on one or two new clues as to who we are.

David Spero, *Untitled #1*, from the 'Aircraft'
series, 1997–1998

WE'RE LIKELY TO TRY OUT many sorts of lives before we land, finally, on the quiet variety. Rarely does anyone start there, the kind of life where we try to be in bed by ten and are intensely grateful when nothing has gone dramatically wrong in the preceding hours. First, we might try out the life of fame, the sort where we dream that someone will stop us in a shop or train station and say, 'Aren't you ...?' or 'Don't I know you from ...' That is a not-negligible thrill, especially if you didn't feel too noticed in childhood and if, in adolescence, it was always someone else who was able to make people you loved smile. Or we might be drawn to the life of melodramatic relationships, the kind where we're constantly wondering whether they love us or we love them, where we break up every couple of weeks and are calling them, frantically, to come back from their parents' house and we didn't mean all those crazy words we said; we were just scared.

It can take a lot of pain before we make our peace with so-called ordinariness and accept it for the wonder it is; before we can deeply love a day when we have 'nothing' to do other than wake up early, finish the dishes from last night, shower, read a few poems, answer some emails, maybe go to the museum to see some African masks or a canoe from Oceania, buy some bread, fry some eggs.

We might become rather fierce at anyone and anything that threatens this hard-won achievement; at well-meaning people who invite us on complicated excursions or to worrying parties; at newspapers that force us to think about driven types starting companies and releasing a new film or record. We know how much these stimulants can cost us.

It takes great confidence to give up on being special. It takes kindness to oneself to interrupt the longing for suffering and anguish. We might need to try out almost everything else before realising, in the end, that it was calm we always really wanted.

Gustav Klimt, *Pear Tree*, 1903

YOU NEED TO RECALIBRATE your sense of the remarkable to remember that this is one of the most valuable and beautiful artefacts ever made, and that if an alien species were deciding whether or not to annihilate us, we could put forward a case that on the sole basis that we made this, we deserved another go.

Until then, so much of art had been overtly dramatic: to bother to justify the price of a picture, it was assumed that there needed to be some angels, some dramatic Biblical moment, or else a haughty aristocrat on horseback with a jutting chin.

But this, very quietly, is a rebuke to all that. It's saying, in its own language, that a quiet ordinary life can be enough, that sitting in the yard, darning a sock, watching over the children, anticipating dinner and talking amiably with a neighbour belong to what makes life truly grand and great. It's a provocation to those princes, battles and divine ecstasies. It is profoundly revolutionary. This painter may be the most famous of his school, but there were a host of others who were engaged on the same magisterial project in his native 17th-century Holland; the re-enchantment of ordinary life. No one had ever lavished so much care on a brick wall or on a cloud. And afterwards, it became easier to do so; there followed hundreds of painters who devoted themselves to turning out quiet scenes: lemons on a table, a jar of basil on a counter or a child sleeping in the nursery.

Still, we ignore them. We say we don't but we do. We pay Vermeer lip service and attend his shows but we don't absorb the deeper message he's trying to send us. That is why seeing his works might make us sad; he is trying to remind us of something before it's too late. But it's too noisy in our minds and in the world and we know we keep losing sight of the true destination: a little street of our own.

Johannes Vermeer, *The Little Street*,
c.1658

THE WORD 'CONVALESCENT' HAS – tellingly and sadly – gone very much out of fashion. In the past, it was an esteemed and highly plausible condition. One had been very ill – and now was no longer quite so. But at the same time, one wasn't entirely ready to rejoin daily life at full throttle either. One was in a precious and fragile intermediary stage: well enough to rise out of bed and do a few things – read a book, answer a letter, peel some peaches – but not well enough to go to a party, run a business or hear disturbing news from outside. One needed – still – protection from life in its most raw form.

We don't need to have been overtly or physically ill to be in need of some of the privileges of convalescence. We have all suffered enough to deserve to count as at some level unwell; we are all delicate enough to be capable of being broken by a few well-aimed blows. It can take only one or two things to destroy us. We have, most of us, known sleepless nights when we couldn't make sense of a relationship, or worried incessantly about the dramas at work, or were so beset by anxiety it became impossible to go out for dinner or to smile without someone asking us if something was wrong.

The designation of 'convalescent' promises us some respite. If we can think of ourselves in such terms, we will appreciate our limits, we won't take risks unnecessarily, we will privilege stability over excitement. We will know how much our steadfastness depends on keeping the surrounding environment steady. We will take care of ourselves and welcome the care of others. The business of living is difficult enough; it can take half a lifetime to realise it isn't weak or indulgent to take very gentle care of ourselves.

Gwen John, *The Convalescent*, c. 1923–1924

ONE OF THE BASIC COURTESIES we almost never remember to pay our worries is to go back and check how they fared against reality. For the nervous among us, no period of life is free of dread-filled apprehensions. One week, we might be worried about running out of money; the next of being sued by a contractor at work; the third about having offended a friend; the fourth of being brought down by a rumour on social media and the fifth about leaving out something key from our tax returns. The worries go on and on, shifting relentlessly from one target to another – ruining our precious time on earth in the process.

What we seldom get around to doing – once the event is past – is pausing to compare the scale of the worry with what actually happened in the end. We are too taken up with the next topic of alarm ever to return for a composed audit.

Nevertheless, if we force ourselves to perform one, a strange realisation is likely to dawn on us: our worries are nearly always completely – and deeply – out of line with reality. Extended out across a year, a 'worry audit' is liable to yield similar conclusions. We almost lost our minds to worry but we didn't – in the end – run out of money; the conflictual work situation found a sound resolution; our friend wasn't

offended, and so on. We might fairly say that only 1% of all the things we ever worry about seem to reach the levels of awfulness we are solidly convinced – in anticipation – that they possess. Mark Twain's famous dictum comes to mind: 'I have lived through many disasters; only a few of which actually happened'.

We should – far more than we do – use the reams of data about the unreliability of our fears as a guide to the future. If we got it so wrong in the past, we're highly likely to get it rather wrong now too. Of course, we're convinced – yet again – that this is really and truly the end, but we were equally certain in a great many other situations that we appear to have sailed through well enough.

Perhaps the world is not – for all its dangers – as awful as we presume. Perhaps most of the drama is ultimately unfolding in a place we need to explore and heal as fast as we can: our own minds.

Edouard Vuillard, *The Yellow Curtain*, c. 1893

THERE WERE — AS IS SO OFTEN THE CASE — few outward signs of what was about to come. That summer, across the United States, the weather was warm but wildfires and periods of extreme heat were few. There were two weeks of almost continual rainfall in the Pacific Northwest. An intemperate grizzly bear caused havoc at Yellowstone after being spotted breaking into a Jeep and making off with the owner's lunch. The stock market reached record highs and analysts predicted a decade of uninterrupted growth. Linkin Park's album *Minutes to Midnight* dominated the charts; the final Harry Potter book, *Harry Potter and the Deathly Hallows*, created long lines on publication; and the celebrity Paris Hilton spent 23 days in jail for violating her probation on reckless driving charges.

What was harder to discern is that this would be the last summer in which any of us would be able to think. The last summer in which we didn't have to know – in enervating detail – everything that was going on in the minds of strangers. The last summer in which we didn't have to compare images of others' lives with our own. The last summer in which we could read a book without stopping to check for messages at the close of every paragraph.

By autumn, the first Apple iPhone had outsold all its less accomplished competitors; by the New Year, it had achieved irrevocable dominance. We never went to bed again without a final consultation. We never started another day without deferring to its auguries. We kept buying books but they ceased to mark us deeply. We were drained of the will to examine the layer of half-formed thoughts on which our capacity for calm and self-direction is based. We went away, but we could never be away again.

We know so much about what technologies give us and so little of what they steal. The summer of 2007 was our last collective summer of mental integrity. We can never uninvent, but we can at least trace back our franticness of spirit to a specific point and thereby start to know and mourn what we have lost.

Chase Dekker, *Horses Grazing, Grand Teton National Park, Wyoming, United States*, 2007

ONE OF THE MOST UNHELPFUL and misleading aspects of chronic anxiety is the certainty it gives us that the true subject of our worry lies in the future. We grow convinced – and insistent to others – that something appalling is on the cusp of happening and scour the landscape for risks, landing on fears about reputation, money, health, looks, employment, or love that fill us with an ongoing sense of eeriness and dread.

·What is concealed in this is a notion as strange-sounding as it may be liberating: that what we might really need to be concerned about may lie not so much in the future as in the past. We may be anxious not, as we ardently think, because we're truly facing anything especially risky right now, but because we have come from a place of immense psychological danger and unhappiness that has wired us to respond to the here and now with a distorted degree of alarm and apprehension.

The catastrophe we fear will happen has, in a sense, already happened – but it has been carefully forgotten in such a way as to leave us with symptoms but no memory of their causes. We carry within us a memory that we cannot put to rest because it hasn't been properly explored and mourned.

We should use the shape of our present fears to guide us back to what may once have saddened or frightened us very badly. We may be so panicked about reputation because we did indeed experience an appalling sense of invisibility in our early years. Our terror that a rival could steal the limelight might be an echo of a dreadful and unprocessed scenario involving a sibling in childhood.

A useful adage tells us: if it's hysterical, it's historical. In other words, high states of alarm almost invariably have their roots in something that happened early on rather than in anything that is threatening us at present. The future will cease to feel so risky once we can take the trouble to explore the traumas on which our personalities have been built.

Vilhelm Hammershøi, *Sunshine in the Drawing Room*, 1910

FOR FAR LONGER than we have been here, upright, in our office chairs, in our well-lit rooms, eating industrially made sandwiches for lunch, we were out there crouching on the ground in caves where, in winter, you had to smash the frozen drinking water with an axe and huddle together in the evening to escape the fears of mammoths and woolly rhinoceroses roaming noisily and angrily outside.

We were, back then, constantly terrified. And for good reason. We were permanently on the edge of starvation. Nothing guaranteed that we would be around next year, let alone tomorrow. We had not the slightest defence against disease and misfortune. In a desperate bid for comfort, we daubed images of the animals we slaughtered in terror on the walls. Survival depended on being able to correctly read the mood of the small band we lived among, but we were never far from the danger of ostracism and abandonment.

Most of all, we learned to be vigilant. Always watching, never at rest. There were no doubt some more relaxed types, but they would have been killed long ago; theirs are not the genes we inherited. We are the descendants of the manic worriers, those who tried to foresee and forestall every possible danger – and lived as a result.

This should make us feel compassion for our situation. Of course we are alarmed; of course we worry too much. How could we not, given where we have come from? We carry fear in our bones. The logical part of our minds was a very late addition. Most of what we are reasons like a very angry fox or cornered wildebeest.

We do our best to see things sensibly and assess risk on reasonable terms. But it is inevitable that we will fail and that late at night especially, when things are as dark as in those early caves, the fears will return with particular viciousness. At 3 a.m. it doesn't matter anymore that there are satellites and key-hole surgery and computers. We are – to all intents – in the ancestral mind, somewhere 17,000 years ago in an underground shelter while outside sabre-tooth tigers howl.

Every alarm may be sounding, but we may not need to pay attention to any of them. We might be able to discount so many more of our fears if we could more regularly remember the frightening places we have all come from.

Depiction of aurochs, horses and deer,
prehistoric Lascaux, France, Upper Paleolithic

IT MIGHT BE A LITTLE EXAGGERATED to say that we go 'mad' if we spend too long in our own company, but we can fairly say that a range of distortions has a marked tendency to creep in.

Over a weekend in solitude, we can allow all manner of suspicions and self-hating insights to become iron certainties. We can end up reasoning in broad brushstrokes. It becomes a fact that everyone hates us, that everyone will find out what we did and that we are talentless, silly and irresponsible. We may get stuck in some very gloomy cul-de-sacs. Nothing is ever going to go right with our career. We'll never find true love.

We should admit that we may not be able to dig ourselves out of this alone – which is a key reason why we need friends. A good friend doesn't have to have a genius-level insight into the human condition to help us. They just need a little common sense and, most importantly, a position outside our heads that gives them a clear view onto things we can no longer see.

To them, and to all fair judges more broadly, there is nothing especially egregious about who we are; we haven't done anything especially bad. We're not heinously ugly; we're not due for a come-uppance or about to be laughed out of town.

We've just let a lot of our fears escalate, and now – perhaps over some tea and noodles in a Chinese diner – we can re-find perspective.

We knew as children how good it felt when a parent was on hand to steady our minds: no, there isn't a lion under the bed. Oh, that's just the wind outside. Don't worry, we'll find your pen or else get you a new one. We haven't lost the need for such basic work of recalibration and reorientation.

We aren't silly to be unable to do this alone. We can be so much more insightful and realistic when it isn't our own lives we need to consider. The true purpose of friendship comes into view: to help us banish the monsters and ogres that breed in solitude and restore us to sanity.

Edward Hopper, *Chop Suey*, 1929

LET'S IMAGINE THAT WE ARE in that particular mood we know as 'irritability'. A drawer doesn't open and we get infuriated. We start banging it intemperately and might rip the handle off its moorings if we were alone in the house. The soap slips out of our hand in the shower and we let out a scream and bang the walls of the cubicle. Someone cuts us up in traffic and we sound the horn for an age until a small child passing by embarrasses us into silence.

We know that something is wrong but not quite what. Somewhere inside us, something very offensive and maddening has occurred but we have lost sight of it – as we will. Probably someone, somewhere, hurt us very much but we have been unable to complain or to realise that they even did so.

But the mind doesn't forget things. It's constantly taking note of hurts and slights and adjusting our mood accordingly. Irritation is anger that forgot where it came from. Just as depression is sadness that lost sight of its origins.

We start to scream at our children when they leave a few toys out because a few hours earlier, at work, we felt humiliated and ridiculed by our colleagues during a presentation. We tell our partner that they look out of shape because, two weeks before, we had an argument about holiday dates and carry within us a subterranean charge of bitterness that hasn't been aired.

We should learn to catch our irritable moods before they motivate us to scream and level insults. We should see them as always being the outgrowth of an emotion that we have not had occasion to process and dissolve.

We aren't in the end ever just bad-tempered or mean; we're furious and sad – and haven't had a chance to say so, to the world (in a gentle way) and most importantly, to ourselves.

Jackson Pollock, *One: Number 31, 1950*, 1950

THE WESTERN INTELLECTUAL TRADITION proposes that in order to be at peace, we need to conquer the world; its Eastern counterpart proposes – more surprisingly – that our time would be far more effectively spent conquering our minds.

That is because it won't matter how grand our achievements end up being so long as our minds are susceptible to all manner of psychological disturbances. The benefits of a fortune are instantly wiped out by depression; a case of paranoia makes a mockery of a luxurious home and a famous name.

The East advises us to stop spending our time trying to rearrange the material building blocks of existence only then to fall foul of psychological ills. We should focus instead on learning how to control and manage the inherently unruly and hugely complicated instrument through which the external world reaches consciousness.

Rather than striving to build empires, we need to spend many years examining how we think and dream. We have to reflect on our families, the economic systems we were brought up under, the impact of our sexual urges and the biological and cosmological order of nature of which we are an infinitesimal part. We have to learn how to breathe in such a way as to allow maximal oxygen to reach our frontal cortex and to hold our bodies so that our organs are not crushed and our blood flow subtly impeded. We need to be able to sleep a regular number of hours and remove all distractions and excitements that might disturb our streams of thought.

This is by no means an easy set of priorities; it is indeed as much hard work as managing a law firm. But the yogis and sages advise that it delivers us a far more secure hold on the actual ingredients of contentment than the bank account of a newly installed CEO with a yacht off Barbuda.

The West has produced too many unhappy playboys, and the East too many genuinely peaceful sages, for us not to think a little about shifting our attention away from conquering the world towards taming our minds.

Attributed to Govardhan, two ascetics from the
Album of Dara Shikoh, c. 1610

NOTHING REVEALS SOME OF THE PARADOXES in our modern ideas of well-being and calm better than the phenomenon of the luxury leisure hotel. At one level, this establishment promises us an unrivalled power to unwind our anxieties and tensions. We will wake up early to walk by the sea, swim laps in the infinity pool, eat light and nutritious meals, slumber on soft sun-loungers and order interesting drinks under the stars. And after a week of cosseting, we will pay the bill with gratitude and relief and return to our lives refreshed.

Except, of course, that a great many of the things that bedevil us outside the well-patrolled gates have a nasty habit of following us inside. Here too we may not be able to sleep. Here too we may regret the divorce and worry about the children. By the edge of an infinity pool, we can fall into a sulk with our partner; we may be silent and sullen throughout an excursion to visit baby turtles; we can eat the chef's speciality while holding back sobs.

The root of the issue is that the luxury leisure hotel operates with an extremely circumscribed notion of the causes of human misery. It implicitly believes that people are rendered miserable by an absence of woven linen, tennis courts and seven-star buffets: in other words, that we are relentlessly material beings who must be cheered by extreme material means. Whereas, confusingly, once a basic level of material satisfaction has been reached, the true causes of our distempers are reliably and predominantly psychological. We ail because we are wracked by trauma, cannot let go of regret, have not understood our childhoods, cannot make relationships work, are out of touch with our authentic selves and are too frightened to be able to be vulnerable with others. And for this, no luxury hotel has any answers; the best concierges fall silent; the most well-meaning establishments struggle to suggest more than a facial.

The luxury hotel is not wrong: the ingredients of calm and happiness are properly exclusive. It is just working with the wrong list. True fulfilment is – sadly – never as simple a matter as titillating the senses. It's a case of making headway with the real and horribly arduous constituents of well-being: a purposeful job, a communicative and kind relationship, three close friends and a capacity for self-understanding. The world still awaits its first 'luxury' hotel.

GG Archard, *Amanwella Resort, Sri Lanka*, 2020

ONCE WE ARE GROWN-UP, we are highly unlikely to think of ourselves as the hero of an epic or fairy tale. Not for us the business of slaying dragons, escaping castles and questing for a prince or princess.

But the curious exercise of trying to turn our lives into an epic or fairy tale might be a rewarding one to take on. *Once upon a time, in a land faraway, X was born ... Their parents were ... When they were Y years old, they realised they had to ...* Our lives invariably offer us plenty of material to work with: we all have challenges we need to overcome, demons that pursue us, lures we have to resist, villains we have to unmask and love we must find.

'Mythologising' our lives generates compassion for something about them we generally ignore at our peril: their inherent and monstrous difficulty. Believing that matters should be relatively easy, we can feel panicked and persecuted when chaos descends, whereas if we view our progress through an epic lens, trials are both dignified and normalised.

Furthermore, when in moments of exhaustion and discouragement, it feels as if nothing adds up – our reversals and loneliness are just so much noise signifying nothing – we can learn to interpret these as belonging within the arc of a story that, though immensely hard, has a basic direction to it. Though we have forgotten to think of it this way, we are – as it were – mid-chapter in slaying a dragon, perhaps of loneliness or inauthenticity; we need to get away from a deceitful prince or princess (we all run into them); we are trying to understand a riddle before it's too late. No wonder we might be tired and scared.

On the outside, we may be living unobtrusively; inside, every life tends to feel closer to the drama and turmoil of the *Epic of Gilgamesh* or the *Golden Legend*. To identify the 'story' we are in gives our struggles logic and shape: divorces, sackings, bankruptcies and rejections can be redeemed once they become staging posts in what we can come to understand as a heroic quest to fulfil our potential and overcome unjust obstacles. We can take pretty much any amount of suffering, once we can find a sense and a narrative for it.

Paolo Uccello, *Saint George and the Dragon*, c. 1470

SO LONG AS THEY ARE NOT OUR OWN and we can keep the experiment to no more than four hours, few things are as relaxing and life-giving as spending time with a child of between 3 and 6 years old.

Children are inherently well set up to remind us of certain vital lessons that we tend to lose sight of, to our great cost, in adult life. For a start, they are ruthlessly honest, as we should be a little more of the time. 'Why is your nose so bulbous?' they will ask us, with understandable curiosity. 'What are farts before they're farts?' They are in touch with their boredom and unbothered by any notion of propriety: they can dare to say that a book or a place are tedious, as we have long ago forgotten to (and as a result ended up wasting a good deal of our lives).

They are cheeringly unmarked by restrictive ideas of what might be normal. We could end up having lunch under the bed or turning the company report into pirate hats. Everything is still a game; that is, an opportunity for an experiment that can be explored without inhibition or fear.

Our small friends are constitutionally unable to hide their emotions. Their faces give us a running commentary on what is actually happening inside them. There are none of the usual boring terrors about being vulnerable: they simply burst into tears or tell us they adore us wherever and whenever the desire strikes them. Their candour lends us a sobering measure of how high we have built our walls – and how cold it is inside them.

They are along the way inveterate enthusiasts. The only people in adult life who can get as excited as they about 'small' things are artists: they will thrill, as Van Gogh or Cézanne did, at daffodils, buttons, jars of pencils and a lemon on the sideboard. Their value system is, as yet, entirely uninfluenced by how much things have cost or how popular they might be. Bubble wrap can be as interesting as a gold watch.

No wonder we feel distinctly restored when we hand them back (gratefully) at the end of an afternoon. These small people are ideal guides to who we have forgotten to be.

Malte Jaeger, *Come on baby, let's conquer the end of the world*, 2015

WE HUMANS ARE ALL, in a variety of ways, experts at 'denial'.

Confusingly, some of these forms of denial are much harder to spot – and therefore to deal with – than others. Sometimes, the manoeuvre is on the surface: someone exhibits a blatant refusal to think or talk about a particular issue or else runs away into drugs or alcohol.

But there are more subtle forms of evasion and one of the hardest to get to grips with is anxiety. We don't typically think of anxiety as a means of escape. Because there are so many genuine things to worry about, it can be hard to see that we may at points be using anxiety in a very particular and psychologically costly way. We are worrying about everything, continually, in order to stop ourselves from understanding, and feeling sad – very sad – about something specific in our pasts. Anxiety has grown into an alternative to self-knowledge.

The dividing line between legitimate concern and anxiety-as-denial is difficult to discern. It can take a long while to see that someone (who might be ourselves) is worrying about money, or their career, or reputation or health in an obsessive and unnecessary way and in lieu of something else: an encounter with orphaned bits of themselves.

What drives the incessant worry about everything is a refusal to be sad about something. We are constantly anxious as an alternative to a reckoning. We are obsessing about certain distinctly unpleasant worries as a way of ensuring that other even more difficult thoughts will stay out of our consciousness.

The way to start to interrupt this pattern of substitute worry is to ask ourselves a very confronting (but not unkind) question: if I could not worry about [fill in the blank], what else might I need to think about?

The question might make us feel confused, thoughtful and sad. We might need to confront a strange idea: maybe there isn't so much to worry about, but there is quite a lot to regret. What may need to replace worry is sadness. The thought, though difficult, is also hopeful. We can be on the path to being a lot less worried once we have gathered the courage to mourn.

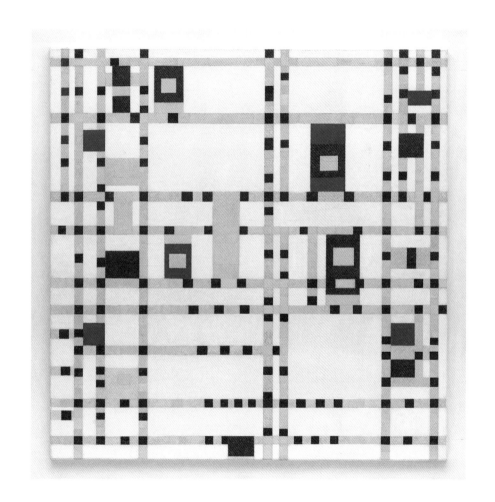

Piet Mondrian, *Broadway Boogie Woogie*, 1942–1943

IT'S EASY TO LAUGH AT THOSE WHO PRAY – when you're an atheist and not too much has ever gone wrong in your life. How ridiculous to clasp one's hands together and beg for help from someone in the sky *who doesn't even exist*; a saviour whom one has only invented out of fear and whom one is relying on a little as a child might their teddy bear. Listen to those desperate innocents mumbling to their mummy or daddy in the clouds.

To which the only robust answer is to say: wait until it happens to you. Wait until your child is diagnosed with a grave illness, your business is threatened with bankruptcy, your reputation is forever shredded, you are condemned, you become known as a laughing stock and you are damned and cursed. And then see how silly it is to pray.

Is prayer really still so daft when you're lying prostrate on the ground in agony? Or might you not have a sliver of respect, and even of desperate envy, for those who don't have to face the worst alone?

At 3 a.m., our heart beating so hard it threatens to burst, crouched on the bathroom floor wailing, we can be proud, still, of our atheism, but very sad about it too. How lovely it would be, at such awful moments, to close our eyes and say: *please, dear Lord, take pity on me, forgive me for what I have done, look with mercy on me, allow me to get through this unharmed, don't punish me as I deserve to be punished. Help me.*

How incautiously sensible we have become with our plethora of carefully reasoned arguments as to why we really are all alone, why death truly is the end and why there can be absolutely no magic and no rescue. How uselessly addicted we have become to mature truths and how hopeless that is when we are at our wits' end. How correct and cruel science has turned out to be.

The non-existence of God should never disguise the fierce longing that a god might exist.

In our deepest crises, we non-believers deserve immense compassion for what we've taken on. We are one of the first generations ever to have tried to get through life on reason alone. Few have ever been so clever – or so brave.

Dmitrii Melnikov, *At prayer in a mosque*, c. 2015

HISTORY DOESN'T RECORD EXACTLY who he is but for our purposes, we know him well enough: he's a very confident young man. And this is principally down to a trait many of us have the greatest difficulty accessing: he doesn't care in the least what other people think of him.

He doesn't give a damn whether you loathe him as a reactionary or dismiss him as a pompous ass. He's not worrying what you might say about him on social media. He doesn't laugh nervously at your jokes or babble in company to try to ensure everyone likes him. He has no great illusions about public opinion or people in general: he long ago understood them to be as dismal as they are. He says what he feels he needs to – and then goes his own way.

We might think him privileged on the basis of his lands, castles and fancy titles but, however nice these might be, they aren't what give him his steely glare or his key advantages. This man has something yet more special and enviable about him than a beautiful horse: he will have had people around him early on who gave him a robust sense of his value. They loved and adored him so much (they would have ruffled his hair and called him 'Aldino' or 'Enzino') that he is now solid inside. It doesn't matter if an ugly article about him runs in the paper or you think he's an entitled jerk; he doesn't need you to approve to feel entirely fine about himself.

A child of a postman and a schoolteacher could, with the right upbringing, also stride the world like a colossus (and several have). Most of us aren't like this because – to an extent we haven't realised – we were brought up on a diet of fear and projected inadequacy.

No one told us we were enough; no one insisted that what 'they' were saying was predominantly ridiculous. Our nervous people-pleasing sides are a legacy of fear we felt about uttering what we actually thought around people with no patience for those who disagreed with them.

It's a great privilege to be born into an ancient aristocratic European family with a castle in the Lombardy plain and a crest dating back to the 9th century. It's an even greater privilege to have the kind of psyche that means you don't need to care in the slightest what others are saying.

Bronzino, *Portrait of a Young Man*, c. 1530s

IMAGINE THAT THE WAITER in the restaurant has brought you the wrong order. You clearly asked for the lamb and here – extraordinarily – are some fish cakes. You might have put this down to an innocent error but something in you resists such an easy interpretation. The waiter clearly has a slightly mocking smile; his eyes carry a trace of sarcasm. This must be a piss-take – and time to get very angry.

Some of the reason why we lose calm so readily is that we jump to the darkest conclusions as to others' motives and see plots to insult and harm us everywhere. We are agitated because we're afflicted by a poignant psychological phenomenon: self-hatred. The less we like ourselves, the more we will appear in our own eyes as plausible targets for mockery and harm. Why would a drill have started up outside, just as we were settling down to work? Why is the coffee not arriving, even though we will have to be in a meeting very soon? Why has someone cut us up at this junction? Why would the phone operator be taking so long to find our details? Because there is – logically enough – a plot against us. And that is because we are appropriate targets for plotting, because we are the sort of people against whom evil things are likely to be directed: because it's what we deserve.

When we carry an excess of self-disgust around with us, operating just below the radar of conscious awareness, we'll constantly seek confirmation from the wider world that we really are the worthless people we take ourselves to be. The expectation is almost always set in childhood, where someone close to us is likely to have left us feeling dirty and culpable. As a result, we now travel through society assuming the worst, not because it is necessarily true (or pleasant) to do so, but because it feels familiar and because we are the prisoners of past patterns we haven't yet understood.

The waiter may indeed have deliberately set out to ruin our evening. But there are many better, firmer – though sadder – hypotheses closer to hand, chiefly that we don't like ourselves very much, because others long ago didn't either. We're not really shouting at the waiter at all: we're shouting at a wretched and unbearable truth about our own pasts.

Gordon Scammell, *Restaurant meals prepared and ready for service*, 2017

WE LONG SO MUCH that it could always be calm. We crave enduringly benign conditions: permanently good weather, still seas, warm skies.

And yet, as meteorologists tell us, flux and disorder are written into the template of the planet. A few days of high pressure must always – by atmospheric law – give way to cooler currents and the release of electrostatic energy and moisture. The oceans will start roiling again. The placid surface must once more turn into an angry grey-green swell.

We can expect nothing less in our own affairs. Expansion and contraction are constants. Entropic forces are perpetually at play. Calm can never be achieved by simply trying to remove every possible cause of external difficulty. The only people guaranteed their rest are the dead.

Calm, in so far as we can find it, must be founded on a distinctive attitude we bring to troubles, rather than any aspiration to remain forever trouble-free. We need to work on healing the traumas in our pasts so that we don't aggravate situations by bringing to them degrees of alarm or anger that they don't deserve.

We need to work on our hopes: well-targeted pessimism is the bedrock of serenity. Nothing more quickly generates frustration than overly high expectations. Of course people will disappoint us horribly; of course we'll be betrayed and maligned; of course most projects won't come off; of course children are a disappointment; of course imagination and kindness are thin on the ground and of course most efforts go to waste. And, closer to home, of course we are idiots; of course we keep making mistakes; and of course we seldom learn.

With such darkness in mind, we should aspire to become melancholy believers in calm who, at the onset of the next disaster, can smile a little and say, very sadly, 'I know, I know'. Nothing need surprise us too much once we have properly understood existence.

We begin life with naive expectations; with time we are so knocked around that we grow filled with rage and frustration. Then – eventually – we may be fortunate enough to acquire realism and serenity. But if we are truly lucky, once we have properly absorbed the chaos of the human condition and said a conclusive goodbye to vanity and pride, we can move on to the last and perhaps best phase: we can start to laugh, darkly and warmly, at the troubled seas we're fated always to have to sail on.

Wolfgang Tillmans, *The State We're In, A*, 2015

Illustration List

p.11 Hiroshi Sugimoto, *Caribbean Sea, Jamaica*, 1980. © Hiroshi Sugimoto, courtesy Fraenkel Gallery, San Francisco

p.13 Michele Nastasi, *Downtown Dubai*, 2015, from the 'Arabian Transfer' series. © Michele Nastasi

p.15 Natan Dvir, *Zara 01*, 2008, from the 'Coming Soon' series. © Natan Dvir/Polaris

p.17 Thomas Cole, *The Garden of Eden*, 1828. Oil on canvas, 97.8 × 134 cm. Amon Carter Museum of American Art, Fort Worth, Texas. Photo Album/akg-images

p.19 *Sleeping baby*. Photo kledge/iStock

p.21 Mark Salamon, *Going Down*. Photo taken 25th August, 2016. From 'Sunsets from the Backyard' series, 2020–present. © Mark Salamon

p.23 Mark Salamon, *Lomo Glow*. Photo taken 20th November, 2018. From 'Sunsets from the Backyard' series, 2020–present. © Mark Salamon

p.25 Giannis Giannelos, *Greece*, 2017. © Giannis Giannelos

p.27 Fujiwara no Teika, *Poems on Flowers and Birds of the Twelve Months* (detail). Edo period (1615–1868), 18th century, Japan. Handscroll; ink and colour on paper, 18.3 × 56 cm. Metropolitan Museum of Art, New York, Mary Griggs Burke Collection, Gift of the Mary and Jackson Burke Foundation, 2015, Acc. 2015.300.25

p.29 Antonello da Messina, *Christ Blessing*, 1465. Oil on wood, 38.7 × 29.8 cm. National Gallery, London. Photo © The National Gallery, London/Scala, Florence

p.31 *Head of a Buddha*, Gupta period (late 5th-early 6th century), Uttar Pradesh, Mathura, India. Red sandstone, 25.4 x 14.3 x 16.5 cm (h x w x d). Metropolitan Museum of Art, New York, Gift of Doris Rubin, in memory of Harry Rubin, 1989, Acc. 1989.236.1

p.33 William Scott, *An Orchard of Pears*, *No. 7*, 1976–1977. Oil on canvas, 63.4 × 76 cm. © Estate of William Scott 2024

p.35 Rachidi Bissiriou, *Jeune Épouse et Mère (Young Wife and Mother)*, 1983. © Rachidi Bissiriou, courtesy of David Hill Gallery, London

p.37 J. M. W. Turner, *The Fall of an Avalanche in the Grisons*, exhibited 1810. Oil paint on canvas, 90.2 × 120 cm. Tate, London. Photo © Tate

p.39 Sunil Gupta, *Charlie and Pablo*, 1985, from 'Lovers: Ten Years On' series. Silver gelatine print, 58.4 × 48.3 cm. © Sunil Gupta. All rights reserved, DACS/Artimage 2024

p.41 Jessica Todd Harper, *Self Portrait with Christopher (living room)*, 2001, from the 'Interior Exposure' series. © Jessica Todd Harper

p.43 Photo © Athapet Piruksa/Dreamstime.com

p.45 Hasegawa Tōhaku, *Pine Forest*, c. 1595. One of a pair of six-folded screens; ink wash on paper, 156.8 × 356 cm. Tokyo National Museum

p.47 The European Southern Observatory's VLT (Very Large Telescope), Unit Telescope 1, Atacama Desert, Chile. Photo ESO/Y. Beletsky

p.49 Albert Bierstadt, *Among the Sierra Nevada, California*, 1868. Oil on canvas, 183 × 305 cm. Smithsonian American Art Museum, Washington, D. C. Bequest of Helen Huntington Hull, granddaughter of William Brown Dinsmore, who acquired the painting in 1873 for "The Locusts," the family estate in Dutchess County, New York. Acc. 1977.107.1

p.51 Johannes Franciscus Michiels, *Bau des Doms, Köln*, 1855

p.53 David Spero, *Untitled #1*, from the 'Aircraft' series, 1997-1998. © David Spero

p.55 Gustav Klimt, *Pear Tree*, 1903 (reworked by the artist 1903/1918). Oil and casein on canvas, 101 × 101 cm. Harvard University Art Museum, Cambridge, Massachusetts. Photo akg-images

p.57 Johannes Vermeer, *View of Houses in Delft*, known as *The Little Street*, c. 1658. Oil on canvas, 54.3 × 44 × 9 cm. Rijksmuseum, Amsterdam

p.59 Gwen John, *The Convalescent*, c. 1923-1924. Oil on canvas, 40.9 × 33 cm. Fitzwilliam Museum, University of Cambridge. Photo © Fitzwilliam Museum/Bridgeman Images

p.61 Edouard Vuillard, *The Yellow Curtain*, c. 1893. Oil on canvas, 34.7 × 38.7 cm. National Gallery of Art, Washington, D.C., Ailsa Mellon Bruce Collection, 1970.17.95. Courtesy National Gallery of Art, Washington, D.C.

p.63 Horses Grazing, Grand Teton National Park, Wyoming, United States. Photo Chase Dekker Wild-Life Images/Getty Images

p.65 Vilhelm Hammershøi, *Sunshine in the Drawing Room (Solskin i dagligstuen)*, 1910. Oil on canvas, 58 × 67 cm. National Gallery of Canada, Ottawa. Photo akg-images

p.67 Upper Paleolithic cave painting of animals from the Lascaux Cave complex, Dordogne, France, estimated to be c. 17,300 years old. Photo Pictures From History/akg-images

p.69 Edward Hopper, *Chop Suey*, 1929. Oil on canvas, 81.3 × 96.5 cm. Private Collection. Photo © Christie's Images/Bridgeman Images. © Heirs of Josephine Hopper/ Licensed by Artists Rights Society (ARS) NY/DACS, London 2024

p.71 Jackson Pollock, *One: Number 31, 1950*, 1950. Oil and enamel on unprimed canvas, 269.5 × 530.8 cm. Museum of Modern Art (MoMA), New York. Sidney and Harriet Janis Collection Fund (by exchange), Acc. n.: 7.1968. Digital image, The Museum of Modern Art, New York/Scala, Florence. © The Pollock-Krasner Foundation ARS, NY and DACS, London 2024

p.73 Indian School, drawings of two ascetics from the *Album of Dara Shikoh*. Attributed to Govardhan, c. 1610. British Library, London (Add Or 3129 f.12r). From the British Library archive/Bridgeman Images

p.75 GG Archard, *Amanwella Resort, Sri Lanka*, 2020. © GG Archard

p.77 Paolo Uccello, *Saint George and the Dragon*, c. 1470. Oil on canvas, 55.6 × 74.2 cm. National Gallery, London. Photo © The National Gallery, London/Scala, Florence

p.79 Malte Jaeger, *Come on baby, let's conquer the end of the world*, 2015. © Malte Jaeger (www.maltejaeger.de)

p.81 Piet Mondrian, *Broadway Boogie Woogie*, 1942–1943. Oil on canvas, 127 × 127 cm. Museum of Modern Art (MoMA), New York, acc. 73.1943. Digital image, The Museum of Modern Art, New York/Scala, Florence. © 2024 Mondrian/Holtzman Trust

p.83 Muslim man at prayer in a mosque. Photo © Dmitrii Melnikov/Dreamstime.com

p.85 Bronzino (Agnolo di Cosimo di Mariano), *Portrait of a Young Man*, 1530s. Oil on wood, 95.6 × 74.9 cm. The Metropolitan Museum of Art, New York, H. O. Havemeyer Collection, Bequest of Mrs. H. O. Havemeyer, 1929, Acc. 29.100.16

p.87 Restaurant meals prepared and ready for service, Newquay, Cornwall. Photo Gordon Scammell/Alamy Stock Photo

p.89 Wolfgang Tillmans, *The State We're In, A*, 2015. © Wolfgang Tillmans, courtesy Maureen Paley, London

Confidence in 40 Images
The art of self-belief

An inspiring curated selection of 40 photographs and artworks with accompanying essays examining the skill of confidence.

The difference between success and failure often comes down to an ingredient that we are seldom directly taught about and may forget to focus on: confidence.

What makes one life cheerful, purposeful and energetic and another less so may have nothing to do with intelligence or qualifications; it may simply be bound up with that buoyancy of the heart and mind we call confidence – the quality that gives us the courage to give things a go, to believe in ourselves and to resist the pull of conformity, fear and despair.

Here is a supreme guide to this fatefully neglected quality; a series of encouraging essays that jog us into a new and more fruitful state of mind. The images that accompany the text are there to ensure that we aren't merely intellectually stirred to change our lives, but that we are also given the best kind of visual assistance.

Although modest in size, this book succeeds at a mighty feat: unlocking our latent powers and edging us on with kindness and creativity to become the best version of ourselves.

ISBN: 978-1-915087-30-0

Self-Knowledge in 40 Images
The art of self-understanding

A visual journey to inspire and guide you through the inward exploration of the self.

When Socrates, apparently the wisest man in antiquity, was asked to define our highest purpose as humans, he responded, 'To know ourselves.' The advice has never been bettered. Without self-knowledge, all other efforts will be in vain.

This is a book to help us on our journey to knowing ourselves better. Made up of 40 images drawn from across different cultures and eras, it takes us on a tour of certain key ideas that we need in order to befriend our deeper selves. Through elegant prose and beautiful art, it helps us to understand how our childhoods have shaped us, what difficulties we characteristically experience in relationships and what our purpose should be.

It will help us in the task of bringing what was once in shadow closer to our awareness, so that we can stand a chance of being slightly less worried or puzzling to ourselves and those who care for us.

Modern society gives us no shortage of ambitions. We will have landed on the one that can finally bring us peace and freedom when we are ready – with the help of this book – to begin the inward journey.

ISBN: 978-1-915087-42-3

To join The School of Life community and find out more, scan below:

The School of Life publishes a range of books on essential topics in psychological and emotional life, including relationships, parenting, friendship, careers and fulfilment. The aim is always to help us to understand ourselves better and thereby to grow calmer, less confused and more purposeful. Discover our full range of titles, including books for children, here:

www.theschooloflife.com/books

The School of Life also offers a comprehensive therapy service, which complements, and draws upon, our published works:

www.theschooloflife.com/therapy

THESCHOOLOFLIFE.COM